DOMESTICALLY CURSED

A Story On Partnership Violence

By Renair Amin

Dedicated to the ones who fought for love but did not have the strength to fight back.

Glover Lane Press
Publishers Since January 2000
4570 Van Nuys Blvd Suite 573
Sherman Oaks, CA 91403
www.gloverlanepress.webs.com

DOMESTICALLY CURSED
A Story On Partnership Violence

Copyright © March 2013 by Renair Amin

Cover Design Provided By Susan Webley-Cox

ISBN-13:978-0615805450
ISBN-10:0615805450

The Mission of Glover Lane Press is to Uplift, Empower, Elevate the Masses and Provide American Jobs. Every book published by Glover Lane Press and its many imprints, is printed and manufactured in the United States of America, ensuring and maintaining American employment.

Table of Contents

PROLOGUE

It seems like just yesterday that I released *Pit Crew: How to Survive a Spiritual Pit Stop*. Truthfully, I did not even know that I would be called upon to write about this chapter of my life and although I would have loved to put every little detail in one book, it appears that each season of my life elicits its own story. I was in the middle of a fast when this book began to speak to my spirit. I tried to ignore it because I was not sure I was ready to open that door.

I get nervous whenever I pull out one of my personal files as I never know what will fall out. Sometimes when visiting the past, you have to be careful not to bring the Ghost of Trauma Past back to life, but there are times when you have to be willing to talk about those experiences in order to help someone else. Whenever I watch television or listen to conversations around Domestic Violence, I find that many of them do not include same-sex situations. I thought that was odd but once I was participating on a panel where it was basically said that "partner violence" situations are often overlooked. I wondered if the reason was because society views two beings of the same sex as equals, there is no recognizable discrepancy around the balance of power and control like in a heterosexual relationship. I also was made aware that in the silence of Same Gender Loving community, we may be erasing our voices from the statistic therefore the severity of the issue goes undocumented which was when I knew that I could not be silent any longer. Although I did change the names out of respect for my past, this story is far from fiction.

I am sharing this story hoping that it will begin to open up dialogue around Partnership Violence. I know that right now there is someone out there covering up their bruises with makeup, hoping to never be exposed. There is someone trying to figure out how to leave while the words, "If I cannot have you, no one will," ring in their mind. Somewhere, there is a spirit who was fooled into believing that "sticks and stones" were the only things that could break their bones. This book is for them. My prayer is that *Domestically Cursed* will open the door for others to talk when they became what went bump in the night.

INTRODUCTION

"They say, I beat my women."

Totally confused as to what her mouth had just uttered, I stared at her. Waiting.

"Excuse me?" I mustered up the strength to ask, hoping I had misunderstood.

"They say, I beat my women," she repeated.

"Who are 'they'?" I asked.

"My friends."

Maya Angelou said "When people show you who they are, believe them, " and here stood this woman honestly telling me her truth but I could not imagine anyone to be that bold. I should have listened because every time the fear would surface, I would revisit that exact moment when I was warned.

I was barely twenty-one when I met this forty-two year old, aggressive woman at a nightclub in Philly. I was out with a friend who kept telling me that she wanted to check out a new club. I indulged my friend since I had not been out in a while. The bar was on the first floor, and the dance party was on the second.

I headed upstairs and that was when I saw her. She was short, light-skinned, with a short Caesar haircut. She was dressed very dapper in some jeans with a dress-shirt, blazer and nice Italian loafers. I saw her eyeing me but I was so nervous. She introduced herself as Chris and I knew in that moment, I had to be with her.

I never returned to the first floor and my friend got very upset and left me. Apparently, this was not just an outing. I was on a date! Shocked that I had been stranded, I suddenly shifted my focus onto how I would get home. Chris and I exchanged numbers and she helped me hail a cab for which she had offered to pay. I was glad because I was drunk which usually happened when I found myself in situations that made me nervous. Liquor was my courage and Tanqueray, my best friend.

Chris was very active so we did not see each other often. Instead we spent most of our time talking on the phone. She regularly pointed out that I was not the only girl that had her attention, but I was determined to change that. She tried hard to convince me that I was too young, which made me press even more. When my mom found out about her, she was not pleased. She warned that someone that much older would cost me. Most of the people that I had secretly dated were older so I ignored my mother. Only this time, she would be right.

When Chris gave her "disclaimer," about her beating women, I assumed this was another one of her ways to get rid of me. She often would throw out little tests to see if I would pass. I kept going because she just seemed like everything that I wanted. I never realized that I was just trying to fill a void. Chris represented stability, wisdom, adventure and promise. These were the things that I desired and I was willing to do whatever necessary to have them. There is a truth to being "careful what you wish for because you just might get it."

DOMESTICALLY CURSED

You lost me yet kept me within your grasp

Crashing my face with your fist

I am a witness to the damage you can do

Question

How does it feel to have a black eye looking back at you

What should I do when you say you love me and shove me

Showing how strong you are

Leaving me scars as reminders

Now I am left to understand how this woman who stands

less than a foot under me can stun me with a threat

Or how her body that's only 120 pounds soaking wet can

defeat me when I stand solidly at almost 300

But cowardly, I just crumble under it as she calls me names

so I can remain in her good grace

I began to hope she would lump my face just to experience

the "forgive-me" side

MY GOD

How I end up on this 3-year ride

With no one to confide in and nowhere to hide

I am just weak at someone else's feet

How did I let her keep me to mistreat me

When it was me

ME

On the phone telling my friends that they were stupid to
get beat by their men
Only to find myself blocking her fists
Twisting from her hits
Trying to have dinner with her when all I want to do is
spit on her
For treating me less than
I even plotted out her murder and what's worse
I BECAME CURSED
Leaving to pass on the insecurities to the next lady
Doing shady things like reacting to subtract from their
worth
And leaving them empty shells to walk the earth
Quick to throw things and be all the things to them that
she was to me
It's like
SHE INFECTED *ME*
And left me with a permanent mirror constantly ridiculing
me
But I accept the responsibility of being the victim in the
first place
For not seeing the truth in her face when she warned me
Or the first time she would scold me
Or the next time her arms would hold me to restrain me
Or The next time her hits would try to change me
Or the next time

Or the next time

Or the next

Next...

Next...

Next... until all that's left is us arguing at the top of the

steps

With her shoving me angrily until I saw my death

So in that moment I became first

But when I finally escaped

I was DOMESTICALLY CURSED

Renair Amin, Reprinted from *Mental Silhouette* (2011)

UNDER THIS ROOF

My mom used to say that if I lived under her roof, I had to abide by her rules. I tried but her rules were *so* different than mine. She wanted me to be the teenager I was but I wanted to be the adult I thought myself to be, so I left. This lasted only a few short years before I had to return back home. Ironically, now I was an adult and her rules really did not match mine. When I met Chris, I had only been back for a short time and my mom was still coming to terms with my sexuality. We had been fighting about Chris almost daily, but I was in love! Whatever Chris said was gold, and anything related to her was platinum. Though I was only twenty-one, so much had already happened in my life. I had been raped, lost two babies, and dealt with a family tragedy. Trying to make it day to day, I was dipping and dabbing in alcohol, cocaine and weed. I had definitely passed the "listening to mom" stage.

After I finally won the tug – of– war between Chris and her other love interest, I was ready to run into my future. Our dating season was short, and after a major blow up with my mom, we began to talk about getting an apartment together. I remembered the disclaimer about her beating her women but nothing alarming stood out to me, so I brushed it off. I also did not pay attention to her subtle threats and put-downs as to how I did things. To me, her controlling ways looked like love to me. *"She was just bossy,"* I convinced myself. That was furthest from the truth. Her mask was falling off.

The concept of the "mask" is an interesting thing. No matter the type of relationship, it usually begins to come off around sixth month. It is right about the moment when you begin to notice the one that you thought was perfect has flaws just like everybody else. This is a normal occurrence, especially if the person is disingenuous; their real personality will have no choice but to come forth.

Having come from a background where I felt abandoned and given away, I desired to have someone love me. When I was very young, my adopted father passed away so my mom was suddenly a widow after forty years which dramatically changed our household. My biological mother was very much a part of my life, but our relationship was strained at times. I spent most of my teenage years trying to find something or someone to validate me. I was often ridiculed for being "book smart," and not "street smart" which was true. I was not able to discern wolves in sheep's clothing. I never even knew they existed. I just wanted to be accepted into whatever club would have me, no matter the initiation.

The abuse started gradually. First, it began with her words. Little questions as to why it took so long to answer my cell phone. If I did not answer right away, she would call me back-to-back multiple times or sometimes she would ignore my returned call. She often felt that she had to teach me a lesson. Sometimes she spoke to me as if I was nothing but a child and since I was only a few years older than her daughter, technically I was one to her.

She did not curse a lot but she spoke in a very condescending, threatening way. One of the things that people have to understand about abusive relationships is that they are about power and control.

One may use things like controlling the money, demanding or withholding sex, checking voicemails and other manipulative ways to tighten the restraints. Before you know it, you have little or no say in any of the decisions that are made in the relationship.

Soon she would begin to inquire as to who I was speaking to on the phone, while determining if I could or could not continue to speak to them. I started sneaking to talk to my friends until it became too much of a hassle altogether. Chris had been systematically rearranging my life but I was too caught up to see it. She even spoke against my living "out and proud." She told me that everyone did not need to know I was a lesbian. She cautioned me as to how dangerous it could be letting everyone "know you were a lesbian" while telling me some of the horror stories of her day. These stories were not new to me as I had heard them from my mom in her quest to get me to understand "what I had gotten myself into." Actually I thought this advice to be funny coming from Chris; she was the poster board for "lesbian," but I listened. *I always listened.* Whenever I questioned her advice, she would say that she was just looking out for my well being. She showed up as my protector and after all I had been through, I believed her. I felt like she was the only one that "got" me. At some point in our lives, we both had been outcasts but together we belonged.

I fought for Chris like she fought for me. Having totally dismissed any naysayers who felt the need to comment on my May-December relationship, I had finally taken a stand in my life. I was more confident. I was loved and that feeling was my adrenaline. Chris became my life. She made me matter. There was nothing or no one able to penetrate our relationship and I was living a dream that was about to end with a slap back to reality.

Our first apartment was a little studio with white French double doors that separated the bedroom area from the kitchen. I loved those double doors, because it reminded me of Paris, a place I so desperately wanted to visit. It was perfect; *everything* was perfect. I was more excited because this was the beginning of our journey together. I felt like there was no where left to go but up. More importantly, everyone had been wrong. She *was* good for me. One particular evening, I had just come in from work, tired and a tad tipsy from a "boss is away" office party at the adult vocational school where I worked. By the end of our party, everyone left a little intoxicated.

I desperately tried to keep my composure while the room swayed back and forth. Chris stared at me oddly but I could not let her know that I was intoxicated because she would have been angry about my traveling in that condition. Searching to see if I had been drinking, she kissed me. The warmth of the Tequila sent me further into her arms. Things were getting rather intense but I needed her to stop because the nausea began to overwhelm me. I drank too much. I went to address her when "Janet..." came out of my mouth. "Who the hell is Janet?!" she snapped. I sat flustered trying to explain that Janet was my co-worker. I could not figure out why I called out her name. There was absolutely nothing going on between Janet and me! Chris' brown eyes filled with flames as her temper began to boil. Sensing something very bad was about to occur, I began backing up on the bed and then she slapped me. It was with such force that my eyeballs felt like they shook. I was shocked. I tasted something metallic; my lip was bleeding. "Is that who you were thinking about while I was kissing you?" Is that why you wanted me to stop?" The questions started coming incessantly now with slaps timed to match. I just covered up my face. She was in full rage and I could barely think, nevertheless block shots. When she stopped I was lying there in a slump, remembering my promise to Janet that I would call her when I got home.

When I was finally able to sob out the reason why Janet's name probably came out of my mouth, it was too late. The damage had been done. Chris just remarked how my blurting out the wrong name at the wrong time made her feel like I was daydreaming about someone else. She never did apologize, feeling her explanation was enough. Not only did I end up apologizing to *her*, I never spoke Janet's name in my house again. This was the first time she had struck me and the day I signed her permission slip.

****

When someone tells you they love you, something changes. If you love them as well, the relationship will begin to move towards the future. If you do not return the same feelings, the relationship will begin to deteriorate unless you are willing to wait to see if something shifts. "I love you" is a phrase that alters things instantly. Similarly in an abusive situation, the most powerful words are "I am sorry." These three words turn the monster into your partner again. You want to believe that they have realized how badly they hurt you. Even if their apology does not seem like one, you choose to accept it. That moment defines the rest of your relationship. If you leave *and* survive their attempts to get you back, you will be free. However, if you stay, you just signed a permission slip for a field trip to hell.

One of the reasons I have heard women say that they stayed, besides their love for their partner, was how nice everything was <u>after</u>. The abuser would buy flowers, offer to take them out, shower them with gifts, etc. They do everything to woo them back and to prove they are truly sorry. Soon your self-esteem takes up residence inside their apology. I hesitate to call it an apology because it does not quite sound like one. Although they may be accountable to how jealous, angry or wrongfully they responded, they definitely will make sure you understand your role in it. Even as the words come out of their mouth, you find yourself at a mental crux. Your lip may be busted or your eyes throbbing in pain, but you slowly begin to feel sorry for *them*. Instead of taking care of your wounds, you are asking them is there anything that you can do to make it better. You know something is gravely wrong with the turn of the tables but you accept them. You also do not want to make them angry again. You move on but never unpack your suitcases because you know it is a matter of time before you are on your trip to hell again.

Sometimes an abuser will try different types of manipulation tactics to make you understand why they hurt you. They may promise that it will never happen again, but soon you realize that it very well could– and it usually does. They may cry and say that they love you so much that when you make them angry, they lose control. When we do not have a proper view of love, this rationale makes sense. Only love this strong could cause them to express so much anger and violence! There is a switch that flips in your mind and you really start to believe you made them do this to you. You keep envisioning the scenario over and over again until you arrive at the conclusion that if you had not said what you said, went where you went, called who you called, or one of the other seventeen reasons that were given, they might not have hit you. Once you not only rationalize but accept their reasons as truth, you have already lost.

The gray area comes in when the abuse is not physical. However, verbal and emotional abuse is equally as bad. There are several reasons why verbal abuse may be overlooked, especially in same-sex relationships. The first is simply that "words can never hurt you." In a society where the word "bitch" has become a greeting among girlfriends, there is confusion around what is considered disrespect. If you grew up in a home where it was not abnormal to be called adjectives such as "stupid," or to be told that "you ain't ever going to amount to much," this type of interaction is normal. These days, chills go up my spine when I hear parents talk to their children in that manner. We cannot allow those types of adjectives to mark our children! Doing so will cause them to believe that not only is it the truth, but others have the right to hold them hostage to those identities as well.

The abuser is usually blind to the damage that is caused to the other person. The abused one starts to isolate into a place where they are petrified to live. There is nothing worse than walking on glass not knowing how or when things could erupt. Over time, the reasons that spark the explosions become more miniscule. After a while you are afraid to even sneeze.

QUARANTINE

Now my relationship with Chris was an interesting one. She had a way of making sure no one knew the other side of her. If I tried to speak on it, people could not imagine her to be such a way. She also was very intentional in the way she structured my life. She did not flat out ban me from hanging out with my friends nor did she make it obvious that she was completely in control of my life. She just subtly began to make the house feel like a place that I needed not to leave, unless I was going work. Instead, we began to have the dinner parties at home. There were becoming less and less reasons to leave the house to have fun. Everything I needed, she made sure I had. We had gone from a studio, to a one bedroom and now we had a house. All this movement was within a two block radius so we were pretty familiar with our neighbors by this point.

The house was beautiful. It was a small newly renovated dollhouse, big enough for the both of us. I was still working at the school and she had gotten a promotion. Since I loved my new home, I did not mind staying in but the arguments had gotten more frequent. To the outside world, we were moving up but inside, I knew that there was a serious alcohol and drug issue arising for the both of us and this did not help matters. I never knew what kind of day to expect. Either we were going to have a great day or a really, really, *really*, bad one.

Aside from the corner bar, my house was the neighborhood hang-out spot. Money was not an issue. There always seemed to be enough money to spend on drugging and partying. Eventually I was happy, simply when she was happy. I was spending less and less time with my friends outside of that. She did allow me to still spend time with my family, but that even had its limits since she only liked certain people.

My drinking was getting progressively worse. It had only been a few years since the murder of my biological mother, grandmother, sister and brother as well as my utopic pregnancy where I lost my child. Since my dating Chris, my mom had disowned me. Plus, never knowing when I would have to participate in *Monday Night Fights*, I was really inside of the bottle to numb the pain. I had been numbing my pain for years so I could not blame her for those issues. However, when you bring two people together that have similar vices for different reasons, it only opens up the possibility that it can get worse.

This was a very firecracker type of situation. We could go weeks without an incident, but when it exploded, there was no turning back. Now the house parties were getting more frequent as were my risks to say or do the wrong thing. Looking back, I now wonder if, subconsciously, I had begun causing fights just to have the "I'm sorry" stage. She was unhappy with some of the recent developments at her job and had become more erratic in behavior. Either she was accusing me of cheating or plotting to leave her but it all was too much. I was slowly entering a place of self-destruction.

By now, I gained about one-hundred pounds from the stress, so the intimacy had been replaced with insults as to how she "does not date fat women." Of course, she never understood that she was part of the reason that I had gained so much weight. It did not matter that we had now been together two years, because every day something new became a problem. I was raised in a home where I was not really required to clean or cook, so Chris considered me a spoiled princess; something she was determined to change. I had to cook a certain way. Act a certain way. Talk a certain way. Clean a certain way. Be all the things, that she needed me to be when she got home from work, the night went very different.

SHAME, SHAME, SHAME

There is nothing harder than trying to explain bruises and marks when you know you are lying. You wonder if your nose is growing every time you say that you accidently injured yourself, making you out to be biggest klutz in the world. There were times that I actually did injure myself especially when I was drinking. I was losing myself. I had very low-self esteem by now with vices to match. It was easier for me to try to survive a hangover than life.

Plus, I was ashamed. My shame was for several reasons. When we met, I stood 5'9" to her 5 feet. During the course of our relationship, she maintained an athletic 145 pounds and I had by now begun to weigh well over 270. I questioned every day how I had allowed this to happen. Later I realized that during the course of our relationship, she had been subliminally replacing my confidence with fear until that was all that was left.

I never knew when I would be embarrassed or chastised. Soon she did not need to strike me because just the thought of it kept me in line. The sad part was that I really loved her. It did not matter if she beat me, because when she tried to make it up to me, she became the Chris I remembered her to be. This would be just enough to tie me over until the next outburst. It is within that "remembering" that holds one inside of the abuse. You convince yourself that if only *you* did not make them angry, everything would have been okay.

You change everything: your friends, schedule, dress, etc. Whatever they need to feel more comfortable, and more secure, you adjust because their peace is your peace. You start to watch for the "look" that tells you when they are getting agitated. You start to listen for what is being said in the silence. You cease to have a good time when you are out because you never know what is being held in the reserve for later.

Another reason I was ashamed was because I had been warned several times. My mother made her case the day she heard Chris' voice over the phone. My good friends had expressed their concerns about some of the arguments they had witnessed. Even my neighbors tried to talk to me. Worst of all, *she* warned me. She flat out said "I beat my women."

All my neighbors knew how bad it had become. I finally worked up the courage to talk to some of the wives who all confirmed that they also heard the screams all the way down the block but chose to mind their business. I remembered the night that they heard those screams. I thought I was going to die.

****

I used to tell her all the time that one day she would accidently kill me. She would stare at me blankly as if that could never happen. Once she had pushed me and I almost fell off the bed into the corner of the night stand. If I had fallen, I would have been badly injured but instinctively she remarked how it was my fault and I made her do it. It was the usual response. Overall, things had been quiet for a while, but I knew something was brewing underneath. *Something was always brewing underneath.*

One day, we had a house gathering with the neighbors. I decided to get some cigarettes so I took a walk to the store. Since it was late and I had been drinking, it was suggested that one of my male neighbors accompany me. I had a feeling that he liked me but dismissed it. I needed someone to accompany me since she would not let me go to the store alone. As we walked further from the house, he began to question my relationship, the age difference and other things that were really none of his business. I felt uncomfortable so I attempted to change the subject. Nothing much more was said until our return to the house. He said he needed to light a cigarette and asked me to stop walking. When I did, he tried to kiss me. Chris always accused me of flirting with everyone, so I knew I could never tell her. I just hoped he would keep quiet and he did but she knew something was wrong. For the rest of the night, I avoided her stares and just kept drinking.

After the party was over, I procrastinated long enough for her to go up to bed. To avoid an argument, I went on the computer and immersed myself in a game of pinochle. I really enjoyed playing but I was a beginner so I would often play online to practice. I was downstairs for about twenty minutes before I heard Chris' slurred words being yelled down from the bedroom asking what time I was coming to bed. I told her I would be up soon and continued playing. About ten minutes later, she called out again. I was becoming annoyed. I was not ready to go to bed. Not only was I high but I was not ready to discuss the evening. After every party, there was a "debriefing" on all the things that I said or did wrong. I was really hoping she would just go to sleep. Usually her anger would reset by the morning, forgetting whatever she may felt the night before.

After about another thirty minutes, I finished my game and shut off the computer. I began to walk up the stairs. The room was quiet and it was pitch black. I assumed she was sleeping. I was not in the bed long before she said, "I thought I told you to come to bed!" Before I could respond, she leaped on me. I could not tell which direction she had come from. I could not see anything. I just felt a barrage of punches. My darkness was interrupted by flashes of light as each blow connected with my face. I just remember trying to block and screaming for help. I did not know my screams would go unanswered as the neighbors sat in their houses, just listening.

BEHIND CLOSED DOORS

In public, we looked happy. In private, I faked it. It got so bad that I had to tell *someone*. There was really no one in my life that I could talk to anymore. My neighbors all had a similarly dysfunctional relationship where fighting and name calling was constant so they were of no assistance. I gave up. Once I had even gone to her friends. Maybe one of them could help her.

One night, midway through our relationship, we were scheduled to go out on the town with a group of her friends. I knew that I needed to have this discussion but I was scared. I was not even sure if her friends knew about the monster that Chris could become, but I had decided as soon as I saw them, I was telling. I figured that maybe, just maybe, someone could talk some sense into her before she killed me.

Chris went to the bathroom and I found myself alone with Jacque, her best friend. I tried to talk as loud as I could over the music but not too loud where everyone can hear. "Jacque, Chris beats me," I said.

She turned, looked at me, and scoffed, "She's still doing that?" I looked at her in disbelief. Apparently this was not a secret and Jacque was not surprised. "She is getting too old for that." That was the beginning and end of that conversation. Later that evening I would end up in the restroom with Sylvia, Chris' ex-girlfriend with whom she was still friends. At this point, I really had nothing to lose so I mentioned it to her. She nicely informed me that Chris was a good woman but that she used to beat her as well. She said she was sorry and hoped it would get better for me. Later that night, Chris informed me that she knew about my conversation with her friends. Jacque did say something to her. She was actually amused. She laughed and said, "Who do you think said that I beat my women?"

Concluding that there was no one who would understand, I accepted the emotional and physical abuse as a characteristic of the relationship. I blocked out the fights and held on for the "good times." When she asked me to marry her after promising to change, I said "yes" hoping that she was really going to get some help. I was the type of person that believed in the "for better or worse" no matter the stage of the relationship. So I gave her the benefit of the doubt that she was really interested in seeking anger management counseling. However, the next time I inquired about the sessions, she shot me such a look that I never asked again.

Her fuse was getting shorter and her verbal assaults more frequent. There was very little that I could say to her that did not get responded to with some type of sarcasm. I have a hard time functioning in situations that are subliminally hostile. I began to talk less and less at home but I had met someone through one of my friends, Tee, who understood what I was going through and had become a listening ear.

I just wanted out. Even though I loved her, the fear that she would kill me was increasing. One day we were arguing and she started to swing on me and I told her that I was leaving. She grabbed me yelling that if I was leaving I was not to wait. She started pulling me towards the door. I tried to break free but at this point she was almost dragging me. She opened the door and literally threw me out of the house. I did not fall or hurt myself but as I turned to go back inside, she slammed the door and locked it. I decided to not sit outside looking foolish. I walked to a nearby family member's home.

I had never told my family exactly what was happening. Some were very fond of Chris and I did not want them to get involved. However, this night I would tell the truth. By the time, I got to the house, I was in crying mess. I told everything. My family was really upset, but I still did not want them involved. Chris must have figured out where I had gone. The next thing I knew, she was at the house promising me that she would never do that again, and I needed to come home. To keep the peace, I went.

The rest of the year would go by without a physical incident but everything else was still the same. My friendship with Tee had gotten stronger and there were developing feelings. I was feeling confused. This was the second time that I had allowed someone in my space. The first time I began to share my fears and concerns with someone, it almost cost my job. They got upset that I would not leave Chris and created a scene in my office. They felt that if I was so unhappy why I would not just come and live with them. It was too much to explain plus I did not want them to get hurt so after the scene at my job, I ended all contact. I was doing my best not to have the same outcome with this friend. I felt like everyone wanted to save me but no one understood, I was not ready to save myself.

I knew I had to leave Chris but I was really afraid. She often would tell me how no one was going to love me the way that she did. I was actually really hoping she was right. I wondered why she held on when all she could talk about was how unhappy she was with me.

It was not long before we got into another argument. I told her I was leaving for good. We were standing at the top of the stairs. She grabbed my arms and started moving me towards the edge. All I could see was my life flash before my eyes. I knew that every argument, punch, slap, venomous word and gesture led right up to this moment. I looked down the staircase. Between the angle and length of the stairs, if she pushed me, I would die. Period.

I had had enough! I got free her grasp and reversed it. Now I was holding her! I just remember screaming, "I am not doing this <u>anymore</u>!" Stunned, she stood there in shock. I did not want to fight, I just wanted to leave. I let her go, walked right down the stairs out the front door and headed back to my family's house. I knew that day that I was not going back. She tried to come and get me but by now I was ready to help myself. I had also been blessed with people that wanted nothing more than to help me get out. I finally told my mom, who I had not spoken to in almost two years, what had been really going on. She asked why I did not tell her. I explained that I been too embarrassed to tell her that she was right so I was willing to die in silence. That was the day we began to heal.

ZOMBIE

I did eventually have to face Chris again. That day was the hardest. The truth was that I still loved her but enough was enough. I actually had been sneaking things out of the house while she was at work. Truthfully, she could have the house and everything in it, except my clothes.

When I walked in the door, I paused. I heard the television. Hoping she just left it on my mistake, I took a deep breath and walked upstairs. Tee offered to go to the house with me but that would have really started a war, so I declined. As I reached the top step I could hear her breathing. I paused. She calmly said, "Hey."

When I walked in the room, she was lying in bed. She was sick. I saw an empty bottle of Puerto Rican Rum so I assumed it was a hangover. It was not. Apparently she had been like this for about a week. She looked at me with a look that took me back to the night at the club. The sadness in her eyes told me she was sorry. She waited to see what my response would be but I simply asked her if she needed anything. My heart hurt so deep but I tried not to show it. She promised to get help. She realized that she needed counseling. She missed me. My lack of response caused her to get annoyed. She tried to make me feel guilty by telling me that I had left her like that for a week and did not care about her. I started to believe her but it quickly passed. Although I loved her, I promised my family, friends and Tee, that I would not go back. I just needed to be strong. I told her that I would come back to check on her, but I did not. I was finally free.

****

I wish someone would have told me how essential it would be for me to heal. I just buried the pain deep while at the same time celebrating my freedom. I started making drastic changes to my appearance. I pledged that I would never allow myself to be controlled again. Anything resembling control was to be eradicated.

I still continued to go get my mail and other necessities but eventually I made arrangements to get the rest of my things and changed my address. Since

I was staying nearby, my former neighbors had taken to informing her of my comings and goings. She was already unhappy with my new look as I had tried to get as far away from who she had once loved. I had cut my hair, changed my dress and started searching for my true self. Eventually she found out about Tee and she kept trying to run into my new beau. However, I could not allow that to happen because someone would have gotten hurt.

I should not have moved on as fast as I did. I just wanted to feel loved again. I needed someone to remind me that I was worth it. *I was not ready to do this work for myself.* Had I healed, maybe I would not have been cursed by the same beast. Instead of emerging a butterfly, I was a caterpillar with a mistaken identity. I could not fly and it did not matter. I had Tee to help me.

Unable to outrun the past, the same controlling, jealous, and insecure presence took over me. I was arguing more and an erratic behavior began to develop. One day I would be so suffocating that Tee could not go to the bathroom alone and the next, I just wanted to be left alone for good. My appetite to stay high was insatiable. I was smoking more weed and had transitioned from cocaine to crack-laced joints. Regardless, I would finish my degree and go on to begin my career. I was a shape shifter. I had mastered hiding myself from the world and I was already in chameleon mode ready to do it again.

Time passed and it would be well over a year and a half before my mask would fall off. Tee and I had moved out of her apartment into a house together. The mask <u>always</u> falls off. It is just the matter of when. I knew that inside I was unraveling but there was nothing I could do to stop it.

Once we had a huge argument while I was eating a piping-hot bowl of home fries smothered in hot sauce and ketchup. I could feel my blood boiling. This was happening more frequently. Although we had never hit each other, we came very close. That night, I was not in the mood. The next thing I knew the bowl of food was being heaved through the air in an attempt to hit her. Before it reached her, it struck the corner of a wall and shattered sending the home fries, hot sauce, and ketchup splattering all around the living/dining room area. Stunned Tee just stood there yelling obscenities refusing to clean up my mess. The bowl shattering snapped me right out of my rage. The grease started forming stains on my "stain-proof" furniture. Tee ran upstairs and I started cleaning.

When she finally came back downstairs, I looked at her. She was still very angry. I apologized and promised that it would never happen again. She forgave me and signed her permission slip. Things did get better for a while. We even had a commitment ceremony, but it was not enough. We had not freed ourselves of our past and soon, more things would be thrown and broken. Drugs became our counselor. The truth was she was not ready to be "married" and I was not ready to be healed. At some point instead of beginning a new life, we had dug up corpses who were now wandering the earth as zombies. We were draining each other's livelihood. When it was over, both of us were domestically cursed.

EPILOGUE

In revisiting this chapter in my life, not only did I have to look at Chris' treatment of me but my responsibility in it all as well. I was operating from a hurt place from the beginning of my relationship with Chris. I was using her to fix my life. Having a void in my life left a space to be filled with what was in my space the most – anger, control, etc. I became my pain, which caused me to do to Tee what had been done to me. When I realized that in order to make me happy Tee had changed her looks, removed most of her friends, and spent a lot of time walking on eggshells. She had become *me*. Although she would later admit that that there were things she could have done to make things better, the truth was that I was not totally healed. Had I been, most of the things that I thought caused us the most strife would have been perceived and received by me differently. Not being healed prevented me from having a healthy relationship I sought.

In every relationship there will be some disagreements, but when most days are full of nothing but control, jealousy, insecurity, belittling, and envy, something is wrong. There is nothing healthy about being afraid to express yourself. When you have to worry about your physical safety on a daily basis, then it may be time to get some help. I risked my physical, emotional and mental health as well as the health of someone I claimed to love. When you refuse to deal with things, they have a way of re-appearing later in life.

I never saw myself as an abuser. I could not admit that I was doing the same damage that had been done to me. Even today, in spite of therapy, I have to be very careful that I never allow that infected area to spread to others. The truth is once you have been exposed, it never really goes away. Just like a person in recovery from alcohol or drugs, they know that they are and always will be vulnerable. Every time I find myself find myself in an argument or a situation that triggers that emotion, I *have* to take a moment. I never want revert back to an unhealthy way of being.

Although the relationship between Chris and I was affected by drugs, alcohol and other contributing factors, the violence was real. I lived that hell in fear of her and what others would think. Know that no one has the right to strike you nor control, threaten or restrain you. Back in school, boys are taught never to hit girls and vice versa. Sadly when it is two people of the same sex, all battles are created equal. She hit me; I hit her back. He called me names; I called him names back. You are to not only hit them back but knock them out! If you find yourself in a verbally, emotionally or physically abusive relationship, know that it is not your fault. Please reach out and get help before it is too late. Your life, soul and being are at stake…

Ask me how I know…

DOMESTIC VIOLENCE INFORMATION AND RESOURCES

LGBT DV

BEYOND THE WHEEL: Tactics of Abuse

Isolation and OUTING—when people are first coming out, *they are very vulnerable to abuse* -they may be losing friends and family, may be alienated from their cultural, ethnic, religious, familial community and institutions. The isolation that most LGBT people face as a result of homophobia *is useful to a batterer* who is trying to isolate their partner. **Threatening to "out" a person (which could mean losing children, ostracism, job loss etc) is a powerful tool of control.**

Using Vulnerabilities—a batterer using their own vulnerabilities to obligate or coerce their partner into staying, caring for them, and/or prioritizing batterer's needs. Using vulnerabilities often results in survivors being exploited (resources, time, attention) and undermines survivors' attempts to negotiate boundaries or prioritize self.

Using Children—In many states, LGBT people are not allowed to be the legal parent of their children. Even in states where LGBT parent's rights are protected, not all individuals have access to the systems to assert their legal rights. For a non-biological parent, the threat of having no contact with their children makes leaving an abusive relationship a complex to impossible choice.

Using Small Communities—Using friends/family and the small number of open and affirming community spaces to monitor a survivor & gather information, to ostracize or threaten to ostracize the survivor. **Please note:** safety planning cannot rely on the survivor never being in community space with the batterer. *Our communities are too small for this.* We must do **harm reduction** planning or survivors "drop out" of community to avoid batterer and risk further isolation.

Leveraging Institutional Violence / Isolation—law enforcement historically and currently have used violence against LGBT people. LGBT people have been targeted for violence in mental health institutions, by hate and bias attacks, and are denied basic civil rights such as the protections afforded through marriage. LGBT people also experience discrimination and oppression based on race, class, national origin, gender, gender identity etc. Many LGBT people, and particularly transgender people, have experienced discrimination within the medical system. **These things are used by batterers to increase control.**

Alcohol and Drug Abuse—LBTG people have historically been forced to make community in" illegal" and marginalized spaces such as bars. We have higher rates of alcohol and drug use and abuse than in mainstream communities. Batterers leverage the ongoing consequences of ways that LBTG people's lives have been historically criminalized AS WELL AS the realities of current drug use (and drug criminalization) when setting up/maintaining a system of power & control.

USED WITH PERMISSION. "*Beyond the Wheel*" *Bullet Points.* This handout developed by Connie Burk ©2005, updated by Kristin Tucker 2009 for The NW Network of Bisexual, Trans, Lesbian and Gay Survivors of Abuse www.nwnetwork.org P.O. Box 20398 Seattle, WA 98102

Domestic Violence in LGBT Community

© 2012 Neighborhood Legal Services Inc., Family Unit
Updated: 7/2012 Page 1 of 2 237 Main Street, Suite 400 ●
Buffalo, New York 14203 ● Phone: 716.847.0650 ● Fax:
716.847.0227 ● Web: www.nls.org

What does domestic violence in the LGBT community look like?

Domestic Violence in the LGBT community looks very similar to the domestic violence/abuse that is prevalent in the heterosexual community. As in the heterosexual community, domestic violence is highly under-reported; mainly because of fear of revealing sexual orientation and the response that might be received from the community.

What are some of the forms of abuse found in the LGBT community?

The forms of abuse are the same among all kinds of people. Domestic violence is the exercise of power and control by one individual over the other and usually includes physical, verbal, emotional, psychological, sexual, spiritual and financial abuse. However, the way that these manifest might be slightly different.

- Threatening you with "outing" thereby exposing victims' sexual orientation, gender identity, and/or HIV status to family, employers, police, religious institutions, the community, or child protective workers.
- Withholding necessary hormone treatment for transgenders, which is medically required during the transition process.
- Use children in common to control you around issues of custody and visitation, particularly in cases where the child(ren) are biologically related to the perpetrator and may or may not be legally adopted by you.

- Constantly reminding you that you will not be able to seek services to escape the perpetrator because of the social oppressions faced like sexism and homophobia. Also, if you an LGBT of color, threats of facing racism when you seek help.
- Terrorizing you that the LGBT in your area is a small community and accusing the perpetrator will let the community make assumptions, thereby limiting your social interactions.

What are some of the common myths in our society about the LGBT community?
- It is assumed that same sex intimate partners cannot be victims of domestic violence because they have equal social standing, are both of equal physical strength and therefore unable to exert power and control over, or be controlled by an intimate partner.
- LGBTQ relationships are abnormal and therefore, the abuse is not serious and the victim should easily be able to leave the relationship.
- Children raised by LGBT parents will become LGBT.
- LGBT parents are more likely to molest/abuse their children.
- LGBT parents cannot provide a stable home for children because children need a "father" and a "mother".

What are some of the barriers to addressing domestic violence in LGBT Community?
- Lack of availability of proper service and trained staff.

- Possible overlooking for LGBT victims by mandatory domestic violence victim screeners at hospitals.
- Most shelters prohibit male victims from entering their facilities.
- When victims in LGBT community come forward, they risk becoming vulnerable targets for general criminal behavior outside of their intimate relationship because of their sexual orientation.
- Most domestic violence support groups are designed for heterosexual victims.

What are some of the resources available to LGBT Community?

- When there is an incident of domestic violence and you call the police, all police officers are required to complete a Domestic Incident Report (DIR).
- Expanded access to Family Court and Civil Orders of Protection to persons who are or have been in an intimate partner relationship, even if they never lived together, got married or have children in common applies not only to heterosexual couples but also to same-sex couples.
- In addition to the family offenses listed in the Family Offense Petition, the police or prosecutor may decide to consider additional charges under the Hate Crime Statute passed in 2000 for violence motivated by prejudice and hate because of race, color, gender, religion, age, sexual orientation etc.

The New York State
Domestic and Sexual Violence Hotline

English: 1-800-942-6906
Spanish: 1-800-942-6908
24-hour, toll-free, all-language Domestic Violence Hotlines that can assist LGBTQ victims of domestic violence with finding support and shelter services statewide.

* Child and Family Service Haven House: (716) 884-6000 [24 hour hotline]
* Pride Center of WNY: (716) 852-7433 [9am-5pm only]

PARTNER/ DOMESTIC VIOLENCE RESOURCES

National Domestic Violence Hotline
1−800−799−SAFE (7233) or TTY 1−800−787−3224

The Northwest Network
The NW Network works to end abuse in our diverse lesbian, gay, bisexual and trans communities. As an organization founded by and for LGBT survivors, we're deeply committed to fostering the empowerment of all survivors of abuse.
Phone: (206) 568-7777

Capital Region Anti-Violence Project
LGBT Domestic Violence Support Line: 518-432-4341.
Aims to help LGBTQ people of color who are victims of IPV.

Equinox Domestic Violence Services
24 hour hotline: 518-432-7865
For information on integrated shelter and services.

Gay Men's Domestic Violence Project
For men in relationships with men
Hotline: 800-832-1901

The Network/La Red
For lesbian, bisexual and transgender women in relationships with women
Hotline/Linea de Crisis: 617-742-4911, TTY 617-227-4911

Emerge
For gay/lesbian/bisexual/transgender batterers
617-547-9879

Violence Recovery Program at Fenway Community Health
For LGBT victims of domestic violence and sexual assault
800-834-3242

National Coalition of Anti-Violence Programs
Information on violence committed against and within the LGBT communities
212-714-1184

The Gay and Lesbian National Hotline
1888-843-4564 or 212-633-7492
Peer-counseling, information and referrals for gays and lesbians.

GLBT National Youth Talk-line
Toll-free national hotline. Provides peer-peer counseling, information, and referral. Available Monday- Friday 5pm-9pm 1-800-246-7743

Safe Homes Project of Good Shepherd Services
Safe Homes Project (SHP) is community-based domestic violence advocacy and service program which provides a hotline, counseling, safety-planning and advocacy for survivors of domestic violence and runs a 20-bed shelter in New York. SHP also provides targeted services for special populations, including Spanish-speakers, youth, and LGBTQ survivors of partner violence
718-499-2151
www.safehomesproject.org

SPECIAL THANKS:

Tyeisha Covington

Susan Webley-Cox

Overseer Yvonne M. Harrison

Azaan Kamau

Rev. Dr. Lisa Robinson

Ketechia "Shye" Sales

Amber Washington

ALSO

The NW Network of Bisexual, Trans, Lesbian and Gay Survivors of Abuse

Neighborhood Legal Services Inc.

Safe Homes Project of Good Shepherd Services

AND

To all the women who have shared their stories…you inspire me

ABOUT
RENAIR AMIN

A prolific author, motivational speaker, and life coach, Renair Amin believes that "Her Voice is Her Purpose" and lives her life accordingly. In 2010, she was awarded the Urban Lyfe Award for Best Spoken Word Artist, as well as named one of the Top 5 Lesbian Entrepreneurs by LezNation Magazine for her work under Pmyner, a creative entertainment company catering to the Lesbian, Gay, Bisexual and Transgender community. Also a licensed Minister of the Gospel at Restoration Temple Ministries, she serves as the Director of the Spiritually Speaking Literary Ministry and Associate Director of the R.A.Y Youth & Young Adult Ministry. Renair Amin is a volunteer motivational speaker in PFLAG's Cultivating Respect: Safe Schools for All initiative, which seeks to provide support, education, and advocacy to students, parents, families, friends, and educators. In addition, Renair is a Certified Life Coach, Certified Relationship Coach, and Certified Spiritual Coach. She is the founder of SPS Life Solutions, a life and relationship coaching company which specializes in helping individuals and couples maneuver life's spiritual pit stops. Renair Amin is the author of the poetry collection, *Mental Silhouette*, as well as *Pit Crew: How to Survive a Spiritual Pit Stop*, a non-fiction self-help book. She currently lives with her wife and son in Brooklyn, NY.

For more information on Renair Amin:

Website:
www.renairamin.com

To contact directly:
spiritualpitstop@gmail.com

"Portions of the sales from this book are being donated to the Safe Homes Project of Good Shepherd Services."

OTHER BOOKS by RENAIR AMIN

PIT CREW: HOW TO SURVIVE A SPIRITUAL PIT STOP
ISBN (10): 0615736726
(GLOVER LANE PRESS, 2012)

MENTAL SILHOUETTE
Poetry Collection
ISBN (10): 0976727331
(DODI PRESS, 2011)

Coming in 2014:

THE IMPRISONED MIND
Break Out to Break Through